the hard questions

JEREMY P. TARCHER/PENGUIN

a member of Penguin Group (USA) Inc.

*New York*

♦

*100 Questions to*
*Ask Before You*
*Say "I Do"*

◆

# the hard questions

◆

# SUSAN PIVER

JEREMY P. TARCHER/PENGUIN
Published by the Penguin Group
Penguin Group (USA) Inc., 375 Hudson Street, New York, New York 10014, USA •
Penguin Group (Canada), 90 Eglinton Avenue East, Suite 700, Toronto, Ontario M4P 2Y3,
Canada (a division of Pearson Penguin Canada Inc.) • Penguin Books Ltd, 80 Strand, London
WC2R 0RL, England • Penguin Ireland, 25 St Stephen's Green, Dublin 2, Ireland
(a division of Penguin Books Ltd) • Penguin Group (Australia), 250 Camberwell Road,
Camberwell, Victoria 3124, Australia (a division of Pearson Australia Group Pty Ltd) •
Penguin Books India Pvt Ltd, 11 Community Centre, Panchsheel Park,
New Delhi–110 017, India • Penguin Group (NZ), 67 Apollo Drive, Rosedale,
North Shore 0632, New Zealand (a division of Pearson New Zealand Ltd) •
Penguin Books (South Africa) (Pty) Ltd, 24 Sturdee Avenue, Rosebank,
Johannesburg 2196, South Africa

Penguin Books Ltd, Registered Offices: 80 Strand, London WC2R 0RL, England

Most Tarcher/Penguin books are available at special quantity discounts for bulk purchase for sales promo-
tions, premiums, fund-raising, and educational needs. Special books or book excerpts also can be created to
fit specific needs. For details, write Penguin Group (USA) Inc. Special Markets, 375 Hudson Street, New York,
NY 10014.

The Library of Congress catalogued the 2000 paperback edition as follows:

Piver, Susan, date.
The hard questions : 100 questions to ask before you say "I do." / Susan Piver.
p.     cm.
ISBN 1-58542-004-2
I. Marriage.   2. Communication in marriage.
I. Title: 100 questions to ask before you say "I do."   II. Title.
HQ734.P72   2000                99-088430
646.7'8—dc2I

ISBN 978-1-58542-621-8 (paperback reissue)

Printed in the United States of America
5  7  9  10  8  6  4

*Book design by Renato Stanisic*

While the author has made every effort to provide accurate telephone numbers and Internet addresses at the
time of publication, neither the publisher nor the author assumes any responsibility for errors, or for changes
that occur after publication. Further, the publisher does not have any control over and does not assume any
responsibility for author or third-party websites or their content.

To my devoted parents,
Julius and Louise Piver,
for spending forty-five years
teaching me what true love and
commitment are;
to Barry Sternfeld, my teacher
and beloved friend;
and to Duncan Browne, for love
that transforms, heals and
brings untold joy.

◆

# CONTENTS

◆

the hard questions

# INTROD

*Loving is a journey with water and with stars,*
*With smothered air and abrupt storms of*
*flour: Loving is a clash of lightning-bolts, And*
*two bodies defeated by a single drop of honey.*
—PABLO NERUDA, FROM SONNET XII

# UCTION

When my husband, Duncan, asked me to marry him I immediately tried to break up with him. We had been together five years, through his divorce, my move to another city, career upheavals, a hostile ex-spouse and a hurt, loving young son. I loved this man. I adored our relationship. But I couldn't imagine promising to love him—or anyone—for the rest of my life. How could such a thing be possible? Every relationship I had ever had up to this point, romantic or otherwise, showed me that *feelings change*.

With great trepidation, I suggested a month of separation to think things over. I went into an intense period of reflection. Wasn't I meant to be an adventurer, a seeker of truth, a lover of men, a captain of industry, all in this lifetime? How could these things mesh with being a wife? How could I follow my heart and soul and still guarantee to love this one, single, solitary man, with all his uniquely glorious, utterly divine, loveable ways *and* his awful, hateful qualities? For all his wonder, he still had only one brain. One spirit. One body. Would they do? For life?

Upon further reflection, I realized I was

holding some fairly bitter assumptions about commitment. Somehow, I believed that once married, I would simply cease living on a certain level. While till now I had been free to roam the earth as my home, marriage would be like confining myself to one room. And someone else would hold the key. No! Never! Not ever! This compromise I would not make, not for love or money or threats of a lonely old age.

After our month apart, after these thoughts and realizations, Duncan and I got together for the weekend. I was ready to lay it all out, without expectation of any particular outcome. I made some speech about how he could never expect me to be a traditional wife, about my commitment to independence and refusal to conform to any external rule of behavior. He listened with complete openness and then, in response, gave me a little box shaped like a heart. Inside it were a rock and a feather. Duncan told me, "The rock is me. You are the feather. Fly. Let me be constant and steady. Let's hold it all in one heart. Let us balance each other." It was a beautiful and complex message. I was in awe of him — of his ability to be loving, to recognize me, to know himself and, shock of shocks, of his willingness to be in a relationship with me, as I am.

As had happened before in this devoted relationship, my love for Duncan expanded to yet *another* level I had never imagined possible. For the first time, it dawned on me that perhaps it was possible to marry and that marriage would actually enhance my life, strengthen me. I realized that the fear I had been holding, the fear of not being accepted for who I am, was immense, indescribable. Duncan didn't help me get over that as much as he supported me in recognizing it.

We spent the weekend in a loving cocoon. When we parted, I knew I couldn't leave this man, that I loved him with all of my heart. But still I didn't understand the marriage vow of constancy. And then, after considering and reconsidering our conversation, I came to the simple realization that enabled me to say yes to his proposal, to marriage. I realized that, no matter how much I might love Duncan right now, I couldn't commit to loving him like this for my whole life, or to sustaining any single emotion of any kind toward anyone for the rest of my life. I would be doing him a disservice by suggesting that I could.

But what I could commit to, what I longed to commit to, what I believed I was capable of, was *acting lovingly* toward him for the rest of my life.

Acting lovingly is a highly complex and

mysterious thing. It is not a matter of always being sweet and nice. It means being radically honest: with ourselves, with each other, with life, forever, in every moment, and dealing together with the emotions that may arise— be they love, hate, boredom, jealousy, ecstasy, apathy or any combination thereof—without leaving. OK, that I could attempt. That I trust. That is a noble endeavor, full of grace. That is worth a lifetime of commitment. And, for me, that is the key to passion.

This book is for anyone desiring a lasting marriage, who also wants an *honest* relationship—and is willing to commit to such honesty above all else, beyond even love. My belief is that this may be the only kind of relationship that can succeed, that can weather the storms and withstand the coves, that can be ardent and secure, all at once.

After my crisis of faith in love, marriage and self, after deciding to marry, all sorts of demonic thoughts began to poke at me: What if Duncan wants to live somewhere I hate? What if I wish we had ten times more money than he wishes for? Is he really OK having another child, or was he just saying so? What if he becomes enamored of someone else? In another fit of insecurity and doubt, I wrote these questions down. The list grew. As I wrote, I realized that there was a third presence in our relationship, that it wasn't just he and I, and that this entity was the thing that could cause our marriage to fail—not any lack of love, passion or agreement about what the marriage commitment should be.

This entity? Our life together. The thing

that we would create to house our love. As I pondered this, as I remembered past relationships, I realized that it was never lack of love that caused the relationships to fail, it was dislike of the life my partner and I had created together. "I love him but I don't love our life together." How many times had I said this to myself? I didn't want this to happen to Duncan and me. Did I really know how this man specifically envisioned his life? His home? My relationship to his son? His relationship to my parents? Our bank account? No, I had to admit. I had only assumptions and hints.

The questions continued to come. I wrote them down. And one by one, Duncan and I answered them, together. Some questions took days to answer. Some took a moment. Others had no answer, and that in itself was important. In every case, we learned something about our relationship and each other. We were delighted, appalled, infuriated and /or mysti-fied by each other's answers. Answering these questions was an extraordinarily fruitful and bonding experience for us. The questions took us everywhere, from the cold, gray heart of disagreement and misunderstanding to the sweet, warm belly of loving intimacy. When we stood up together in our marriage ceremony, we knew, as much as we were able, what we were saying and whom we were saying it to. When I looked into Duncan's eyes and said I would be his wife, I felt it was the most honest promise I had ever made, one offered from the very center of my heart, directly into his.

## *How Answering the Hard Questions Can Help You Make a Powerful Commitment*

In this book, you'll find many of the questions Duncan and I answered, plus more, gathered from friends, strangers and colleagues. If you are in (or desire) a committed relationship, full of passion *and* safety, this process can help you achieve it. If you are looking for ways to honor the commitment of life partnership with someone you love, without giving up who you are and what you dream, this book is for you. And, if you feel, as many do, that "no matter *what*, I don't want to get divorced," answer the Hard Questions.

We enter marriage offering the best of who we are: our deepest feelings, our best intentions, our greatest hopes, full of generosity and affection for our partner. But we fall in love and decide to live the rest of our lives together without realizing that loving each other and loving our life together *are different*. This book is about envisioning your life together, with great care, consciously. It is about skillfully balancing the crazy wisdom of love with the grounded practicality of making a life together. It is about the middle road, the constant, meaningful interplay between these two extremes, loving a person and loving the life you create together. Strong marriages exist comfortably here, between the fire of intimacy and the ground of pragmatism.

In the past, there was little need to create a shared vision of married life. Couples had a vision handed to them: the husband will work, the wife will tend the home, they will go to the same church on Sundays, try to be monogamous, buy a home, have kids, send them to college, etc. Now, nothing is a given. Husbands may not work. Wives have careers. Committed couples may not be married or even live together. Adoption is wonderfully common. Husband and wife may attend separate churches (or temples, shrines, lectures, support groups), or attend none at all.

For those of us contemplating marriage in the new millennium, a conscious effort is required to create a shared vision. Nothing can be taken for granted. There are no cultural models for us to look to. Often, traditional religious values can't support our relationship. For many of us, our divorced parents can't offer a model to emulate. TV, movies, music: They're all about easy solutions, romantic escapades, youthful passion. How, then, to create an adult view of relationships, one that includes passion and commitment, the fullness of who each person is and can be?

Marriage is often presented as a relationship that naturally runs out of passion—or one that requires all sorts of work to maintain—scheduling time for sex (yuck), taking workshops, going on special vacations, etc. Isn't it possible to have a long-term, committed relationship, full of energy, naturally passionate? I could not imagine entering marriage without believing that it is. I want full-on emotional, sexual, spiritual passion—not the torments of fights and jealousies, but the power of engaging deeply, from the bottom of my heart, with my lover's heart, with lots of ebb and flow in both passion and friendship, periods of great agreement and great distance, but always coming back to each other, to self, to commitment, together.

There is no technique, no gimmick, no class, no easy answer. The solution, the *only solution*, is knowing and revealing yourself and receiving your partner—relentlessly, and with great skill.

*The Hard Questions* helps create a shared view of life and a deeper knowledge of yourself and your beloved. It can be used throughout the life of a relationship; answering these questions ten years into a relationship is as valuable as answering them ten months into it. The questions can be useful whether your committed relationship is one of marriage or not. They can be answered by straight or gay couples and are not predicated on any particular religious beliefs. Whether used as an ongoing tool or the basis of a single conversation, within the context of a committed relationship or as a tool for self-knowledge, the Hard Questions can help lead to a deeper level of intimacy.

It is important to recognize that each of your answers contains important information about who you are, what you believe, how you were raised and what you value. No matter how simple the answer may appear on the surface (e.g., $50,000 is how much income we need to earn), once you scratch the surface, you will find a reservoir of powerful emotions and deeply held beliefs. When your partner gives an answer that sparks anger or fear in you, it is important, *crucial*, to put those emotional responses on hold, even if just for a moment. During that moment, if you can try to understand your partner's own internal logic, you will both benefit tremendously. No matter how odd or inappropriate or silly you find your partner's response, I guarantee that, to him, there is a powerful, important set of reasons for it, reasons that *matter*. Your work is to understand your partner's internal logic.

This process is powerful. It will blow away half thoughts and codependent fantasies. It will uncover addictive and neurotic behaviors. It asks that you accept it all. It asks that you be open to truly *knowing* your beloved. It asks you to show yourself, allow yourself to be known. This is not for the faint of heart. But if you are seeking a marriage based on true intimacy, not romantic fantasy, if you are interested in a relationship of equal partners, if you want to relate and be related to emotionally, spiritually, physically, intellectually, then this difficult but incredibly rewarding process is exactly right for you. Ultimately, through revealing and accepting self and other, through paying attention to your love affair *and* your life together and always working to tell the truth, a genuine long-term romance is created, a relationship that is at once profoundly secure *and* full of energy: one that can last a lifetime.

Don't try to answer all the questions in one sitting. It may take days, weeks or even months to fully answer these questions. Each of you will need paper and a pen, nothing more. Each time you are ready to approach some of the Hard Questions, find a safe space and some time when you won't be disturbed. Sit with your beloved in a place that is relaxing and peaceful for both—your bedroom, the dining room table, a restaurant, a park bench, on a long drive. The important thing is to minimize distractions. If you are at home, turn off phones, beepers and computers. You may want to play music that is special to you both. If you have children or roommates, wait until they are asleep or out.

If it is useful, you can set a time limit on the discussion, such as: "Let's devote thirty minutes [or one hour, or two days] to focusing on these questions, and no more."

First, practice knowing your own answer. As you begin with the first question, take some time to understand your own response, without speaking it, or thinking of what anyone's response may be. You may even want to take some time with the questions on your own, before beginning with your partner. In any case, become clear about what your real, truthful feelings are, as clear as you are able to be.

Each question should be answered by both of you, one at a time. When you are both ready, one of you may begin answering the first question you have chosen. It may take a moment or an hour. Allow each person to answer fully, without interruption. Each person may take as much (or as little) time as needed. It is important for the listener to simply hold the space for the speaker by looking at him, listening to him, fully, till the end. You can sit close together, holding hands, or apart, across a table. Whatever enables you to focus and concentrate is what you should do.

Try to listen completely, with as little judgment as possible. As questions, emotions and thoughts arise, set them aside. Try not to relate to them. Try to continually open up more and more space in your own mind and heart for your partner's answers. Your own judgments and responses, while crucially important, will take up too much room right now. Trust, really trust, that they will still be there when you need them. They will.

If there is agreement between your response and that of your partner, write out the shared answer in a notebook or piece of paper that you have set aside for just this purpose. "We both see $50,000 as an appropriate combined annual income for ourselves." Then move on to the next question. When you have finished answering the Hard Questions, you will have important answers about making your life together happy, at this moment in time. Save these answers, whether you have agreed, disagreed or drawn a blank. Keep them in a special place, perhaps in a beautiful binder or together with other sacred mementos of your relationship. Feel free to revisit the answers or change them together anytime. Life changes and so will the answers to the Hard Questions.

It is wonderful when you and your partner agree on the answer to one of life's Hard Questions. But one thing our culture doesn't teach us is that it can be equally wonderful when you and your partner disagree. We tend to fear disagreement; our minds come up with so many stories about what disagreement means. "We're not right for each other," we think. "My life will be made miserable by her." "He will eventually leave me because of this." "I will have to become someone I'm not in order to continue living with her." Ultimately, disagreement conjures the expectation of failure. Very scary.

But if we work with our minds, we can arrive at a place where disagreement means none of these things. We are accustomed to believing that discomfort is bad, should be banished and disposed of by whatever means available. It's true that discomfort doesn't feel good, but if we can find a way, within ourselves and together, to hold off, even just for a moment, from running from discomfort, it will bear gifts. The nature of disagreement is discomfort—but discomfort just means that a boundary is being stretched.

What does this mean on a practical level? It means taking no position in a disagreement. The moment I say, "You are wrong and I am right," the dialog between us is dead. It is key to continually express your own feelings *without* making pronouncements about your partner's feelings, needs and desires. "When you say that $30,000 is an adequate income for our family, I feel really scared of living in poverty" is quite different from "$30,000 will never be enough for the life I want to live." The former invites intimacy and dialog; the latter is an ultimatum. Even if one partner never wants to do more than $30,000 worth of work, he can most likely empathize with his mate's fears about poverty. If each can find a way to acknowledge the validity of the other's feelings, there can be a conversation. Even if a couple ends up disagreeing on the specific outcome, they will have evolved their relationship, their knowledge of the other, to a deeper level.

The most essential tool in the answering of questions, both difficult and easy, is kindness. True kindness is an extraordinary combination of soft and hard, simple and complex. It can be held through disagreement, pain, anger, even unkindness—without sacrificing any part of the truth of your feelings, responses and needs. This sort of kindness enables you to be yourself, to show yourself and to receive the truth of your lover, with all his qualities, beloved and detested.

True kindness is the ability to open your eyes, ears, mind and heart to the fact of what your beloved is saying and feeling, of *who your beloved is*. On good days, you will be delighted by him, his mind, his intentions, his desires. On other days, you may be appalled, terrified, disappointed, bored. In each instance, it's vital to hear him, without denying his truth out of your own fear and insecurity. It is important to always love *him* a tiny bit more than you love your relationship with him, to hold the truth of his heart and soul with great gentleness and spaciousness. This is a very soft and loving thing to do.

To do this, you have to be in constant, uncompromising contact with your own responses, the aforementioned fears and insecurities. True kindness involves a rock-hard commitment to honesty, to knowing and revealing yourself. This is the only way to separate your partner's words from your feelings about them. When discussing the Hard Questions about each other's job aspirations, for example, your partner may express a desire to leave his well-paying-but-going-nowhere job for a more risky but potentially satisfying possibility. This may arouse feelings of discomfort in you. Why? Explore the discomfort and try to differentiate it from the decision facing your partner. Perhaps it brings up fear that the new job will introduce your partner to a new community of people. But "When you talk about wanting to switch careers, I'm afraid you'll fall in love with someone else" is different from fear of a risky new job. It's incredibly easy to confuse the two. It's important to understand your fear so that you don't discourage your partner's opportunity out of some general, unnamed fear of change.

First, there is the awareness of discomfort

when the new job is spoken of. That is yours. Then there is the meaning of the new job for your beloved. That is his. Both are crucial to discuss. There is no rest, no break, no vacation from this discipline of knowing yourself and receiving your beloved. It is very, very hard.

Once you have fully heard your beloved's perspective, considered what he is saying apart from your own needs and reactions, then it is time to let them all come flooding in. Tell him what they are. It's totally possible to have a thorough conversation with your lover about his new job: the pros, the cons, the logistics, the needs it will fulfill for him—and then tell him, "OK, but I absolutely hate this, I am terrified, I can't bear the thought of you making this change in our lives." And then it is his turn to hear you and to receive you. Holding two different vantage points on the same issue can be very complex—but endlessly rewarding.

Ultimately, what choice do we have in communication that isn't manipulative or unconscious and numb? You speak. You are heard. He speaks. He is heard. And on it goes. When you have something very difficult and potentially frightening to say to someone you love and care for, you begin by saying, "I love and care for you and I have something very difficult and potentially frightening to say." And then you say it. In that sense, communication is really quite simple.

For Duncan and myself, our first wedding vow was, "I vow to know and receive you deeply and with compassion." This is the commitment: to know each other and to receive each other. To be known and received. How much I have longed for just this, to be together with my husband in this place of endless relating to the natural ebb and flow of emotion, desire and personality. Is this not the ultimate kindness?

*Chapter 1*

# HOME

Our home is the most immediate expression of who we are and how we view life. It is the place we retire to after giving of ourselves in the world all day long. It is the one place in the world that should be safe space. It is the location, for many of us, of what-we-do-besides-work, i.e., hobbies and creative endeavors; the pursuit of dreams that may have nothing to do with workaday efforts to secure income and achieve status; the place where we long to unfold, be ourselves, show the world who we are and share our lives with those we love most. In addition, for many of us, home is the most tangible manifestation of financial and emotional security.

Marriage often begins with agreeing to share a home—to share the financial burdens of maintaining it, the joys and hassles of decorating it, the creation of a way of living *together*. After the ceremony, after the honeymoon, the newlyweds *go home*. Even if they lived together before the wedding, this particular trip home is different. *Now we are a family. Now we are here to stay. Now my things are also yours. Now your clothes on the floor mean something different and are particularly terrifying. Is this what I will come home to every day? Let the fears begin. . . .*

It's crucial to discuss the space you and your partner will live in together. Form can give rise to content. No matter how much you love each other, the feeling and properties of the space you share will affect the course of your relationship. A small space may feel cozy to you but suffocating to your partner. Casual housekeeping may denote relaxation to your partner and slovenliness to you. It is important to hear your lover's needs on these topics, and to express your own.

The delineation of physical space may stem from the way the two of you delineate psychological space. Do you require a lot of privacy, separate from your mate? Do you require space to work at home? Does the majority of your communication take place at the table? In the bedroom? What your home looks like, how much time is required to care for it, how much of your income goes into creating and sustaining it, where it is located—the answers to these questions reflect deeply held assumptions about life and the future. We often begin envisioning our homes when we are still small children. "When I'm grown up, my house will have a swimming pool in every room" may have morphed into "I want a Jacuzzi in the master bathroom"—but still, the Jacuzzi will be emblematic of a long-held desire. It's good to uncover and share these desires, no matter how unlikely they appear in the cool light of adulthood. And remember: Your home is where you live with your beloved, but it is also where *you* live. Whether or not you have the luxury of space, your home needs to shelter both the couple and each individual—on all levels.

These questions will help you and your beloved clarify your views of home.

**1.** What does our home look like, physically? Outside? Inside? Any particular style (modern, traditional, etc.)?

**2.** How many rooms should there be and for what purpose will they be used? For example, what is important for me/us to be able to do at home (relax, work, make love, study, meditate, play guitar, be with friends)? Make time to describe rooms that are particularly important to you (e.g., kitchen, bathroom, family room).

**3.** Describe the feeling you want to have when you walk into our home. What makes you feel secure, happy? Would you like our home to be peaceful and spacious, with no evidence of the outside world? Full of laughter, warm light and coziness? Complete silence? Neighbors and friends coming and going? Both? Neither?

**4.** Where is our home? Describe its geographical location. What surrounds the house? Neighbors? Trees? Shops and museums? The ocean? A gated community? Acres of undeveloped land?

**5.** What is it? Apartment? House? Townhouse?

**6.** Who is responsible for keeping our house and yard (if relevant) cared for and organized? Are we different in terms of our needs for cleanliness and/or organization? Is one or both of us neat? Messy? A "pack rat"? An organizational wizard?

**7.** Who is responsible for grocery shopping, cooking and other tasks connected with meals? Do we eat out? A lot? A little?

**8.** What do we sleep on? A king-size bed? A waterbed? A futon? What else is in our bedroom besides the bed? Let yourself dream about where you will dream. . . .

**9.** What percentage of our income are we prepared to spend to purchase and maintain our home on a monthly or annual basis?

**10.** How much will we spend on furnishings? Who will make these decisions? What factors are important in making these decisions (price, quality, style)? Do we want to be free to re-decorate as our tastes change, or do we expect to invest in quality that will last a lifetime?

**11.** How long will we live in our current or first home? One year? Ten years? Forever?

**12.** Do we have a sense of our own style? Do we care? What is my style? Ours?

**13.** Who may also stay there or live there? Do we have any roommates or tenants? Do we have pets?

**14.** What is my wildest fantasy about our home (e.g., an outside shower, all-white décor, wild-animal preserve, three guest rooms)?

*Chapter 2*

# MONEY

Of all the subjects couples can discuss, money is the most metaphoric. Money can mean security, love, power and/or freedom. Perhaps because of its various levels of meaning, it is one of the subjects most often battled over. Financial disagreements cause probably as many failed relationships as do sexual/romantic disagreements. It is almost guaranteed that each partner holds undiscovered assumptions about money, from "My husband will always support me" to "Separate checking accounts mean a lack of trust."

It's important to examine them all—but almost everyone I know cringes at the thought of discussing money. I know much more about my friends' sex lives than I do about their financial situations. Money is often the final frontier in terms of intimacy between two people.

Growing up, I had no idea how much money my family had. I still have no idea. We never talked about it—and yet we talked about it all the time. "That's too expensive." "Money doesn't grow on trees." "It's very important to save." "You have to learn the value of a dollar." "We're taking away your allowance." "We're giving you $50 for your birthday." But somehow, it never seemed quite real. I have yet to learn about money: how to amass it, invest it, save it, grow it. And I suspect I'm not alone. For many people, money is the most unconscious, terrifying subject of all; many of us never master it.

Marriage brings to light special financial hopes, dreams and fears. For some women, no matter how independent, there is a sense of wishing *at last* to be cared for financially by a husband or partner. For some men, a culturally ingrained sense of needing to provide for and take care of the family rears its head at the time of commitment to a relationship. These great unconscious cultural archetypes—women provided for, men providing—are never manifested as vociferously as on one's way to the bank.

There's nothing wrong with embracing the traditional view. However, it's vitally important to be conscious and clear about your expectations. Problems arise when one model ("We are equally responsible for our finances") is espoused, while another model ("Take care of me!") is *felt*.

**1.** How much money do we earn together? Now? In one year? Five years? Ten years? Who is responsible for which portion? Now? In one year? Five years? Ten years?

**2.** Are our current combined salaries enough to cover our expenses?

**3.** What are our categories of expense (rent, clothing, insurance, travel)? How much do we spend monthly, annually, in each category? How much do we *want* to be able to spend? Now? In one year? Five years? Ten years?

**4.** What is our ultimate financial goal regarding annual income and when do we anticipate achieving it? By what means and through whose efforts?

**5.** How much money do we have in our checking accounts right now?

**6.** How much money do we have in our savings accounts right now?

**7.** How much money do we have invested or saved elsewhere (stocks, annuities, retirement funds)?

**8.** How much money should be in our savings account so that each of us feels "safe?" How much do we contribute to it monthly or annually? Who makes these contributions, and in what proportion?

**9.** Where do we put our money (bank account, mutual funds, retirement plans)?

**10.** Do we keep our money in joint or individual accounts?

**11.** What kinds of purchases must be jointly decided upon?

**12.** How do we decide how to spend our

money? Is there an amount ($50, $500, $5000) over which we need to discuss a purchase before committing to it?

**13.** Who keeps the household books and pays bills?

**14.** Who does long-range financial planning (retirement, investments)? How are these decisions made and who implements/tracks/manages them? How is life insurance secured? In what amounts? Who are the beneficiaries? Do we have pre-existing investments and if so, will any changes be necessary after marriage?

**15.** If we have dependents from a previous relationship, what part of our finances goes to them, now and in the future? When unpredicted financial events occur involving them, what is the new spouse's involvement/input/ responsibility?

**16.** How is health insurance secured? Does either of us have existing health needs, concerns or conditions?

*Chapter 3*

# WORK

Work can be the center of our lives or simply the means to an end, or both. In any case, outside of family, work often houses our most important relationships. Professional relationships and goals can have a powerful impact on the life of a couple. Often, men and women hold quite specific views of their spouse's work ("My wife will never/always have to work," "My husband's work will never/always support us," "My travel and time needs for work will often/never take precedence over family commitments," etc.). It's important to examine these assumptions and confirm or deny them with your partner.

Most likely, both partners will require each other's emotional and/or financial support to reach their professional goals.

Perhaps you expect your partner to participate in social events with you and your coworkers. Perhaps you require your partner's understanding while you socialize separately with coworkers. Or perhaps the support you require from your partner is not social at all in nature: You may need him or her to listen to your ideas and actively participate in your creative and professional development. You may require the opposite: plenty of space and privacy to work through work-related thoughts and problems. Like most of us, perhaps you require all of the above at various times in your professional life.

What are your current work needs? Answering the questions below can help you and your partner clarify feelings about such important topics as ambition, expectations of support and commitment to your own and your partner's professional goals.

**1.** What are our separate professional goals in terms of position or job desired? One year from now? Five years? Fifteen years?

**2.** Is each of us content with our current jobs? If not, why?

**3.** How much time will each of us spend at work, and during what hours? Do we begin work early? Will we prefer to work into the evening?

**4.** Outside of the office, how much of our time are we willing to put into work? What place does the other's job have in our home life? Do we have an office at home? Do we bring work home? How much time is spent working at home?

**5.** What is our relationship to the other's work? What do you expect of me in terms of support, encouragement and relationships with your coworkers?

**6.** If one of us doesn't want to work, under what circumstances, if any, would that be OK?

**7.** How ambitious am I? How ambitious are you? Are we each comfortable with the other's level of ambition?

**8.** How do I need you to support my professional/work goals? Do I need time and space to explore my creativity? Do I need financial support? Do I need your advice? Do I need time and money to attend school or receive additional professional training?

**9.** When, if ever, do we want to retire? Where would we like to retire? How would we like to spend our time after retirement?

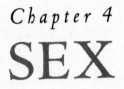

*Chapter 4*

# SEX

The erotic, sexual connection. It lives. It dies. It is reborn. Or not. What aspect of a relationship is more mysterious than this? Where do trust and passion and anger and adoration and need and ennui live most directly between you and your partner?

Perhaps we marry for romance. Perhaps we marry for security. Perhaps we marry to start a family. Perhaps we marry because it is time to do so. Perhaps we marry because we have found our soul mate. No matter. Ultimately, we end up in bed naked with the person we have married, no matter what got us there or what we imagine marriage to be about.

Then what? The body is incapable of lying. Even when it behaves unexpectedly, inscrutably, it is still telling a truth, albeit a truth born of its own internal logic. I believe that who you are *is* who you are in bed. This is the place of most glorious intimacy, horrible treachery and stinking boredom, which makes it the most fun, the richest *and* the likeliest place to numb out. Your sexual relationship with your beloved is a place of powerful honesty, like it or not. Who can bear that for very long? Who can bear to be without it?

Over time, you and your partner will undoubtedly notice that your levels of desire don't always match. You want to. He doesn't. You are in the mood for something wild and aggressive when he wants to linger and go slow. How do you meet in the middle? How do you even *know* what your partner is in the mood for? Do you ask? Do you offer silent clues? If you have already developed your own language, some combination of talking, gesturing, grabbing and sidling up, do you like the way these communications go? Are they accurately rich? It is worth spending some time figuring it out.

In a new relationship, sexuality is often (elegantly and/or inelegantly) experienced only while making love. As you live together and learn each other, you see your partner's sensual nature expressed in many ways: the careful way he prepares a meal, his aggression at the gym or on the highway, the sweet way he cares for children, his love of beautiful fabrics or single-malt scotch. All are expressions of an erotic connection to life and living. As time passes and you remain together, continue opening up to each other, the initial sexual intensity can become beautifully displaced from the bedroom into every aspect of your lives together. Being together becomes erotic.

"The more I am with my beloved, the deeper our erotic connection will become." This leaves room for the lovely thought that the older I get, the sexier I may become, *to him*.

Longevity, commitment, knowing, being held by this knowing and for this knowing: This is sex as home, as the finest way we are given to express and receive love, lust and each other.

In answering these questions, feel free to be poetic, shy, definite or embarrassed. Try to speak accurately, as earnestly as you can, as much as you are able. Go slow. Help each other out. Get down with the truth. Find satisfaction and help your partner find satisfaction.

**1.** Am I comfortable giving and receiving love, sexually? In sex, does my partner feel my love for him or her?

**2.** Am I affectionate enough with my partner? Do I cuddle and cherish him or her enough?

**3.** Am I comfortable giving and receiving lust? Does my partner feel how much I desire him or her? Is our sexual connection satisfying on a purely physical level?

**4.** Are we satisfied with the frequency of love-making? How do we cope when our desire levels are unmatched? A little? A lot? For a night? A week? A month? A year? More?

**5.** What if one of us is attracted to someone else? Superficially? Deeply?

**6.** How do we each deal with the sexual expectations and needs of the other? What does one expect of the other in terms of sexual safety and exploration? Can I be deeply honest about my fantasies and longings and not do damage? If damage *is* done, then what?

**7.** Is there a spiritual aspect to our sexual relationship? If so, how might it be expressed or honored?

*Chapter 5*

# HEALTH
## AND FOOD

Attitudes toward food and the ways we eat, shop, prepare and serve it are wonderfully reflective of deeper values, as are attitudes toward exercise, body image and aging. For some couples, grocery shopping, preparing meals and dining out are a source of relaxation, a way to continually court each other, a time to reconnect and relax. Mealtime is often *the* time of family togetherness, especially if a couple has children. Without children, it is often the time that a couple spends "decompressing" or creating romance and togetherness. Some people find food and the act of dining together to be one of the great sensual joys of life. Fine wines, gourmet cuisine, excellent conversation: These are time-honored sources of pleasure. Others consider such things to be a nuisance, an expense, inexplicably complex.

There can be great satisfaction in being extremely formal or extremely casual about food. If you were raised that dinnertime is precisely at seven, and reserved for strict conversation about current events, as an adult you may find it delightful to watch TV and eat pizza. It's important to make note of these things.

In addition to pleasure, the way we prepare and eat food bears direct relation to the way we care for our health and looks. When you are sick, what makes you feel taken care of? What do you eat to maintain your health? Do you take great care with the foods you eat or are you happiest ordering in fast food? The way we feed and care for ourselves and others, in sickness and in health, speaks loud and clear about what makes us feel nurtured. When I was sick as a child, my mother would bring me toast and tea. To this day, toast and tea make me feel better, no matter what I have learned in the interim about caffeine, fat and glycemic indices.

For most of us, eating treads the line between science and art. We may find it very important to adhere to a certain diet—out of ethical, cultural or religious beliefs, or for purposes of weight control, cancer prevention, enhancing energy or controlling a chronic health condition. We may consider the act of preparing and eating food to be an expression of pure delight, or feel that paying attention to the quality of food is a sign of hopeless narcissism or new age propaganda.

Exercise and physical fitness play important roles in making ourselves look and feel good, sexual, relaxed. Many of us are plagued by dissatisfaction with how we look. We put ourselves on fitness regimens to lose weight, retain youth and vigor, stabilize moods and fight or prevent chronic health conditions. If physical fitness is important to one partner but not the other, it may cause resentment about time and expense. If I pride myself in being fit and trim, how will I feel if my beloved doesn't take care of his health? If he gets fat, will I still feel good about his body? It's helpful to think about how your attitudes may differ, and what conflicts may arise over food and health as time goes on.

**1.** Do we eat meals together? Which ones?

**2.** Who is responsible for food shopping?

**3.** Who prepares the meals?

**4.** Who cleans up afterward?

**5.** Does either of us have special dietary concerns or needs relating to weight, health, etc.?

Does the other agree with or support these needs?

**6.** How much time do we spend exercising? How much time do we *want* to spend?

**7.** Do we each feel comfortable about our current levels of fitness and health? Are there any areas (weight control, cholesterol levels, muscle tone, flexibility) that are of concern to one or both of us?

**8.** Does either of us have health concerns (e.g., chronic conditions such as high blood pressure, diabetes, asthma or illnesses that run in the family)?

**9.** Do the health, dietary and/or exercise needs of one or both of us require any life-style adjustments or changes? Any special financial expenditures?

**10.** Do we each feel supported by the other in these areas?

**11.** Is each of us happy with our overall health? Where could there be improvement?

**12.** Is each of us happy with the other's approach to health? Does one have habits or tendencies that concern the other (e.g., smoking, excessive dieting, poor diet)?

*Chapter 6*

# FAMILY

Relationships with your partner's parents, siblings and/or children can reveal deep truths about where you place value in personal relationships. I may believe that all family members are welcome in our house at any time of day or night, while my spouse may feel that three A.M. is not an acceptable time for visitors of any sort, even a sibling in crisis. I may wish to invite my mother over to discuss decorating questions; my partner may view this as intrusive or overly dependent. It's valuable to examine assumptions like these.

Many of us retain into adulthood unresolved issues with our families of origin—issues which we may attempt to resolve, consciously or not, within the context of marriage. If you have a parent who is alcoholic, for example, you may refuse to keep liquor in your home, but your partner may enjoy having a drink when he or she comes home from work. Can you or should you separate your deep feelings about alcohol from your partner's needs?

Today's families are often complicated, involving parents, stepchildren, ex-spouses, extended families, long distances and unresolved issues. Whether a family is nuclear or fragmented, ferocious feelings can be provoked by one partner's criticisms or judgments of the other's family. It's important to look carefully at the dynamics in both partner's families of origin and try to deal with any deeper issues each person may possess.

**1.** What do I like about my family of origin? What do I dislike?

**2.** What do you like about my family of origin? What do you dislike?

**3.** What is your current relationship to my family? Do you like this relationship? Are you close? Do you desire more or less closeness? Do they desire more closeness from you? Are you comfortable with my parents and siblings?

**4.** What place does the other's family play in *our* family life? How often do we visit or socialize together? If we have out-of-town relatives, will we ask them to visit us for extended periods? How often? For what length of time?

**5.** If we have children, what kind of relationship do we hope our parents will have to their grandchildren? How much time will they spend together?

**6.** What holidays and events do we feel are important to spend with our family of origin? Do we give gifts? Do we have special celebrations? If so, what is involved and where are the celebrations held?

**7.** What holidays and events are important for *our* family to observe? How do we celebrate and what kind of time is spent celebrating each other's birthdays? Our anniversary? Our children's birthdays? Our relatives' birthdays, anniversaries and special events?

*Chapter 7*

# CHILDREN

I know some couples who have agreed never to have children. I know others who want to have them right away. I have known some who have felt strongly one way or the other, then changed their minds. This is hardly surprising, since few decisions in life are as important as whether or not to have children.

Childless couples hear all sorts of stories from their friends who are new parents: "We are completely sleep-deprived." "We never make love anymore." "We are depressed." "We can't stand to be away from our baby, even to go to work." "We had no idea how drastically our lives would change." "Our baby is driving us insane." "We are completely in love with our baby." "We never have time to spend with each other anymore." Having a baby is the most natural thing in the world—yet nothing can prepare you for life as parents.

Friends of mine in their late thirties recently became pregnant while on their honeymoon. They definitely wanted to have children and knew they had little time to waste. But while they were ecstatic to learn of their pregnancy, they also really missed having had time to be alone together as husband and wife. In your relationship, do you want to have plenty of time to get to know each other and establish a household before having children? Do you want to have children right away? If nature allows, it's wonderful to consider such questions while you still have the ability to make choices.

Another friend once said to me, "Having a child brings you face to face with the best and worst of yourself." Both she and her husband are exhausted by the demands of their beloved year-old baby. My friend is testing the limits of her patience, selflessness and energy—as well as the limits of her relationship. The other day, her husband came into their bedroom having left their daughter shrieking in her crib. "I just told Suzie to *buzz off*," he said to her, ashamed. They stared at each other and, luckily, burst out laughing. No matter how long a couple has been married, when they have children they get to know each other in a different way.

In addition to lifestyle changes, questions about raising and caring for children can evoke powerful, half-consciously held opinions about religion, discipline and education. Many logistical and philosophical questions arise about providing child care, teaching values, establishing routines for eating, playing and doing schoolwork, instilling religious or spiritual beliefs and administering discipline. While it is impossible to anticipate exactly how you will feel once you have children, it is important to prepare for it by discussing your beliefs about raising them early in a relationship. And if you decide that you don't want children, since our society still finds it difficult to accept childless couples, it's important to discuss how you will respond to the inevitable questions asked by friends, relatives and strangers.

**1.** Will we have children together?

**2.** If so, when?

**3.** How many?

**4.** How important is having children to each of us?

**5.** Is it necessary or desirable to consider adoption, infertility counseling or genetic testing?

**6.** How will having a child change the way we live now? Will we want or be able to take time off from work, or work a reduced schedule? For how long? In the months or years following the birth of our child, will we need to rethink who is responsible for housekeeping?

**7.** When our child is a baby, will she/he be breast-fed? For how long? Will we adhere to a strict feeding schedule or not?

**8.** When our child is older, will we try to enforce any particular dietary habits (limit sweets, prohibit processed foods, encourage vegetarianism, etc.)?

**9.** How will we instill discipline in our child?

Lectures? Yelling? Spanking? "Time Outs"? Is one of us more naturally a disciplinarian? How will we handle our disagreements over administering discipline and teaching manners and values?

**10.** How much time will each of us spend with our children?

**11.** How much time will we spend without our children, just the two of us?

**12.** Who will take care of our child if we both work? How does each partner feel about daycare?

**13.** When our child is older, will we limit access to TV, music, computers or reading material, based on content? What type of content do we find objectionable? What sort of

TV, music, computer games, Internet content or reading material will we encourage or discourage? Will we set time or viewing limits on TV? On time spent playing video games or surfing the Internet?

**14.** Will we raise our children with any particular religious or spiritual beliefs? If so, how will we do this? Will we give our children a religious education or expect them to participate in religious rituals (observance of Sabbath, religious holidays, confirmations, Bar/Bat Mitzvah, etc.)? What will we teach our children about big issues such as God? Suffering? Birth? Death?

**15.** If we decide not to have children, are we both completely comfortable with the decision? What if one of us changes his or her mind?

Regarding children from previous relationships:

**16.** How much time will we spend together?

**17.** What does the birth parent expect in terms of his/her child's relation to the stepparent? What does the stepparent expect? What role, if any, will the new spouse play in the care, discipline and education of her partner's child?

**18.** What is the child's physical and emotional space in the new family and home? What special care needs to be taken to assure his/her comfort and security in the birth parent's new relationship?

*Chapter 8*

# COMMUNITY AND FRIENDS

One of the great complaints of modern life is lack of community. Whereas our parents or grandparents may have been born into a community, most of us have to consciously create one. A contemporary couple's life is often full of micro-communities, based around work, working out, hobbies or spiritual or cultural pursuits. Community can also come from specific friendships: With these people we do sports; with these we talk about books; with these we go to parties. Both partners bring to the relationship a set of existing friendships; new, historic, dysfunctional, meaningful. Because it's not always easy for one's beloved to naturally fit into the other's existing communities and relationships, it is valuable to take a look at them one by one and see where the possibilities for deeper community or the risk of distress lie.

Whether or not a specific community is sought, we often wish to sustain or create meaningful friendships outside of our primary romantic relationship. It's valuable to check in with your loved one about his take on these relationships. Does he appreciate them for their enriching qualities? Is he threatened by them for the time they take you away from him? Do you view this as charming or irritating?

Aside from existing communities and friendships, one of the exciting things about being in a committed relationship is the opportunity to create new communities and friendships *together*. Whether such ties are religious, spiritual, cultural or revolve around sports or hobbies, shared community and mutual friends provide a chance for you and your beloved to root your relationship outside of your personal home. It is an opportunity to create an expanded sense of home.

**1.** With whom do we socialize as a couple?

**2.** How do we meet new people?

**3.** Are we satisfied with the quality and quantity of friends we currently have? Would we like to be more involved socially? Are we overwhelmed socially, and do we need to cut back on such commitments?

**4.** Was one or both of us born into an ethnic or religious community? What role, if any, does this community play in our life together?

**5.** What kind of community do we envision ourselves in? Close-knit? Occasional get-togethers? Based around work, religion, cultural pursuits or hobbies? How do we achieve that community?

**6.** Which of us is responsible for creating community? Is one partner more outgoing than the other? Does one partner have a greater need for outside friendships and groups?

**7.** Do I appreciate/resent the way my partner interacts with my friends? Of my existing friendships, do any seem particularly wonderful or threatening to my partner?

**8.** What are my partner's needs for cultivating or maintaining friendships outside of our relationship? Is it easy for me to support those needs or do they bother me in any way?

**9.** Do we belong to or support (with money and/or time) any charities or causes?

*Chapter 9*

# SPIRITUAL LIFE

For many of us, religion is something that we observe when someone is born, marries or dies. Suddenly, at such moments, the religion you were raised with, the traditions your family may have followed, become vitally important. Any impulse your beloved may have to devalue or ignore such traditions can become very, very hurtful. It's important to examine what you will do, if anything, to mark the passages of life, including death. If you are married, it is likely you encountered this curious arousal of attachment to tradition while planning the marriage ceremony.

Also, for many of us, spirituality has become increasingly important in our day-to-day lives. Many people have "practices": yoga, meditation, communal gatherings, discussion groups, that are central to their lives. Is it important to share such practices with your beloved? If so, why? If not, why not? And what happens when one partner holds childhood religious traditions dear while the other has created a unique spiritual practice, totally apart from the religion he or she grew up with? How are both belief systems honored and blended under one roof?

**1.** Do we share a religion? Do we belong to a church, synagogue, mosque or temple? More than one? If not, would our relationship benefit from such an affiliation?

**2.** Do we share a spiritual practice such as meditation, yoga or some other type of "nontraditional" observance? If not, would adding such a practice enrich our lives together?

**3.** Does one of us have an individual spiritual practice? Is the practice and the time devoted to it acceptable to the other? Does each partner understand and respect the other's choices?

**4.** What does each desire of the other in terms of support and/or participation in the other's practice?

**5.** How do we mark births and deaths within our family?

**6.** What place do spiritual and/or religious beliefs play in our home and home life?

**7.** Do we observe any spiritual rituals? Celebrate any religious holidays? Together? Separately?

**8.** Will we be buried? Where? If not, what do we want to happen to our bodies?

# AFTERWORD

◆

Entering marriage can be a commitment to the unending enlargement of Soul, instead of an unnatural limiting of self. "With you, I will become who I truly am" is much more passionate and courageous than, "In order to be with you, I will narrow who I may become, and try to fit your picture of who I should be." In any case, the latter promise can never be kept. It must shatter. The former is not the commitment to love forever, but the commitment to *act lovingly* forever: This is a profound and worthy commitment, full of grace.

Passion and commitment. They go together. What a relief.

I hope that answering the Hard Questions together with your partner has helped you make a commitment that will last a lifetime, and I wish you the best in undertaking this powerful process. May you live in love and be transformed by it.

# ACKNOWLEDGMENTS

◆

For their kindness, friendship and feed-back, I would like to thank Josh Baran, Peter Baptiste, Samuel Bercholz, Thomas and Maricel Brown, Julia Cameron, Bette and John Cooper, Howard Cushnir, Joel Fotinos, Robert Gass, Glenn and Carol Hanna, Bill Horwedel, Wendy Hubbert, Diane and Ron

Katz, Cyndi Lee and David Nichtern, Joan Oliver, Richard Pine, David and Zea Piver, Harriet and Howard Shrier, Chalo Smukler, Helen Tworkov, Eliot and Louisa Vestner, and Andrew Weil.

A special, endless note of thanks to Dr. Barry Sternfeld for his essential contributions in crafting this book. His remarkable intelligence, compassion and humor infuse its spirit, as they do mine.